The House by the Sea

SELIMA HILL

 Fair Acre Press

First published in Great Britain in 2022 by Fair Acre Press
www.fairacrepress.co.uk

Copyright © Selima Hill 2022

The right of Selima Hill to be identified as the author of this work has been asserted by her in accordance with the Copyright, Designs and Patents Act of 1988. All rights reserved. A CIP catalogue record for this book is available from the British Library

ISBN 978-1-911048-62-6

Typeset & Cover design by Nadia Kingsley

Cover photo © Maisie Hill 2022
www.maisiehill.co.uk

About Selima Hill:

Selima Hill "has won lots of prizes, and not won many more. She lives by the sea in Dorset with her dog and a bald robin."

Books by Selima Hill include:

Women in Comfortable Shoes, forthcoming
Men who Feed Pigeons, 2021
Gloria: Selected Poems, 2008
Bunny, 2001
Violet, 1997

Death is Superfluous.
Death is entirely Superfluous.

Daša Drudic, Doppelgänger,
translated by Celia Hawksworth.

*A stone man riding a young crane
flies over the blue mountains.*

Kusan Sunman, Korea.

Contents

9..... This is Where She Died
10... The Person in the Chair
11... Two Boys
12... Nobody is Here
13... Mice
14... The Sea
15... Roses
16... The House is Full of Stones
17... Anything That Breathes
18... Murdered Kings
19... Ducks
20... Pebbles
21... Afternoon
22... The Bed
23... The Doctor
24... Moons
25... The Person's Face
26... The Crunch of Boots
27... The Mole House
28... Praise the Muddy Ducklings

This is Where She Died

This is where she died
and since that night
everything is buried
under stones,
nothing can be seen
except the stones
that dedicate their lives
to being motionless.

The Person in the Chair

The stones have come
and buried everything
and nothing can be seen
of the chair
and nothing can be seen
of the person
who finds he can't get up
from the chair
and anyway
it's his favourite chair
and he can sleep
as much as he wants to,
the sitting-room
is completely full,
it's like a glass
full of cold milk.

Two Boys

Upstairs in the bedrooms
heavy stones
are burying the bodies
of two boys
as if a beach
has slipped inside the house
and wrapped itself around them
as they sleep.

Nobody is Here

Nobody is here
except the stones
and those who rest
underneath the stones,
those who have lain down
and taken refuge
underneath and inside the stones,
the fearless stones
that have outgrown the sea.

Mice

It's no good mice
hoping for the best
and praying they'll be spared
because they won't,
the stones are specially trained
in crushing mice,
the smaller
and more terrified
the better.

The Sea

What did they,
the boys,
even look like,
has anybody told them
they can't move,
has anybody told them
that the stones
have come upstairs
because they miss the sea?

Roses

I think I have offended the stones,
they're burying the roses
and the sheds,
they've colonised the kitchen
and the dining-room,
they're piling up
against the window panes,
and will they break the glass,
of course they won't,
they're much too cool
to go around breaking things,
they're here to watch,
to coach,
to make us still.

The House is Full of Stones

The house is full of stones,
completely full,
everything is buried
under stones,
they're weighing down the sofa
and the beds
and, on the beds,
the bodies of the boys,
they weigh them down,
they're stones made of sea,
the sea has come inside
and stopped moving
and in the silence of the house
the stones
congratulate themselves
on being ruthless.

Anything That Breathes

The bodies of the boys
are not moving,
they seem to be listening
to the stones
talking to each other
in the dark,
talking about how,
as stones,
they specialise
in burying
anything that breathes.

Murdered Kings

They may be smooth
as reinvented fruit,
they may be tears
re-emerged as weight,
as patient
and as secretive
as eggs,
but they are stones
and they have murdered kings.

Ducks

They spend their days
doing nothing much
as if they want to burst into tears
but don't know how
or what will happen next
and bursting into tears, for a duck,
is unacceptable,
they've got to wait,
and sooner or later a person
will come into the garden,
wring their necks
and suffocate himself
in the feathers
that press against his purple mouth
like gas.

Pebbles

It makes them sound like babies
but they're not,
they're deadly serious
and they object
to being called pebbles
by old fools.

Afternoon

Nothing will distract him
from the stones,
their shoulders in his lap,
their thick grey lips.

The Bed

The person hurts,
he hurts
but not with pain,
he hurts with the embrace
of his sorrow
that holds him tight
and tells him
that eternity
is waiting for him
like an unmade bed.

The Doctor

It's only a matter of time,
the doctor says,
how many are there,
and they're not boys,
they're men, for Heaven's sake,
before the men
re-emerge
like mammals
from their tunnels,
their wonder
like small mammals'
snouts
in roots.

Moons

They shine like moons,
like beautiful beached moons,
they shine because to shine
is not to flinch,
to pay the price
that those who grieve
must pay,
the price that must be paid
for having loved.

The Person's Face

The person's face
is buried under stones
whose weight
is causing bruising
and swelling
but somebody will come
to lift them off,
somebody
he can hear tapping.

The Crunch of Boots

In the sun-burnt garden
the roses
abandoned their petals
to the bugs
that scattered
when they heard
the crunch of boots
as two unsmiling men
with a stretcher
made their way
across the bone-dry lawn,
the crunch of boots
that sometimes he remembers
and sometimes he will find he will forget.

The Mole House

And sometimes it can happen
that the stones
start to feel soft
as if each stone
has grown a velvet mantle
like a mole,
as if the house
is a mole house
where moles in hundreds
come on holiday
with sleeping-bags
and cake
and more cake.

Praise the Muddy Ducklings

Praise the muddy ducklings,
praise the ducks,
praise the roses
as they fall apart
and praise the god of worms
and praise the worms,
praise the tiny birds
that praise themselves
and hop about
as if nothing's happened,
praise the mourned
and praise the hungry mourners,
praise the salmon,
praise the salmon mousse.

Lightning Source UK Ltd.
Milton Keynes UK
UKHW020401050123
414828UK00011B/186